# Understanding CATS

## Bridget Gibbs

First published in 1978 by
Usborne Publishing Ltd,
20 Garrick Street,
London WC2

Text and Artwork © 1978 by
Usborne Publishing Ltd.

All rights reserved. No part of this publication may be reproduced, stored in a retrieval system or transmitted in any form or by any means, electronic, mechanical, photocopying, recording, or otherwise, without the prior permission of the publisher.

Published in Australia by Rigby Ltd, Adelaide, Sydney, Melbourne, Brisbane, Perth.

Published in Canada by Hayes Publishing Ltd, Burlington, Ontario.

Printed in England by
A. Wheaton & Co Ltd,
Exeter

**Written by**
Bridget Gibbs

**Consultant Editor**
Patricia Scott, M.B.E., Ph.D., F.I.Biol., of the University of London

**Additional advice from**
Peter Messent, M.A., D.Phil.
L. B. Halstead, Ph.D., D.Sc., of the University of Reading

**Designed by**
Sally Burrough

**Illustrated by**
John Barber, Colin King and Sam Peffer

Silver Tabby

Seal-pointed Siamese

# Understanding CATS

## About this book

This book will help you to understand how cats behave and how to look after a cat of your own. It explains why cats do curious things like eating wool and what it means when a cat swishes its tail or flattens its ears. The book also looks at the parts of a cat's body and shows how they work and what happens as a cat gets older. The chart at the end of the book shows lots of different cats to spot.

## Contents

| | |
|---|---|
| The world of cats 4 | Growing up 22 |
| A cat's body 6 | A new pet 24 |
| Cat language 8 | Looking after your cat 26 |
| Hunting 10 | Kinds of cats 28 |
| How cats behave 12 | Cats to look for: |
| Intelligence and learning 14 | Shorthairs 30 |
| Watching cats 16 | Longhairs 31 |
| Courtship and mating 18 | Index, Books to read 32 |
| The birth of kittens 20 | |

Red Self

# The world of cats

The domestic cat belongs to the animal family called Felidae, which includes all cats from large ones such as lions to smaller ones such as lynxes. Cats are carnivores, or meat-eaters. All carnivores developed from a weasel-like ancestor called Miacis.

The cat-like animals that descended from Miacis, which lived on earth millions of years before man, were the ancestors of all the cats we know today. No-one is quite sure how cats eventually came to be tamed, or domesticated, but it is likely that they have been associated with man from about the time he started farming. The ancient Egyptians, who lived about 4,000 years ago, may have been the first people to be aware of the cat's usefulness. They probably started to feed cats as a reward for ridding their homes of mice, which were eating their grain.

The cat family are hunters, relying on stealth and speed to catch and kill their prey. Several features enable them to be excellent hunters: they have supple joints, powerful muscles, special teeth and sharp, retractable claws (see page 7).

About 50 million years ago, a small weasel-like creature called Miacis lived by hunting prey in the forests. It was the ancestor of all living carnivores.

An animal called Dinictis developed, or evolved, from Miacis about 36 million years ago. It looked a bit like a lynx, and had cat-like teeth and claws.

All present-day cats belong to the cat family (Felidae), which evolved from Dinictis. The wild cat shown here lives in European forests.

The domestic cat is probably descended from the desert cats of Egypt and Arabia. These cats tame easily and would accept domestic life more readily than any others.

## Big cats

The cheetah is the only cat which has claws that cannot be retracted (sheathed) when they are not in use.

Most cats except lions prefer to live and hunt on their own. Lions live in family groups called prides.

### Skulls and teeth

The sabre-toothed tiger, called Smilodon, was a descendant of Miacis and lived about the same time as Dinictis. It, too, was a carnivore and it had enormous canine teeth for catching and killing prey. Like Dinictis it had eyes and ears well placed at the front of its head for detecting prey.

Modern cats, including the domestic cat, have essentially the same features as their ancestors for catching, killing and eating prey. They have forward facing eyes, a strong hinged lower jaw, large, sharp canine teeth and tearing carnassial teeth.

# The cat's skeleton

A cat's skeleton is made up of about 230 bones which are worked by about 500 muscles. Unlike dogs, whose skeletons vary considerably in shape and size, all domestic cat skeletons are very similar. They are lightly built and so flexible that, unlike humans' limbs, the cat's limbs do not get put out of joint.

Cats walk differently from other animals. Their front legs swing inwards so that the feet land in a line, one in front of the other, directly under the cat's body. The hind legs do not swing in quite so much, but the footprints still nearly overlap. This is why cats can walk along fences and narrow ledges.

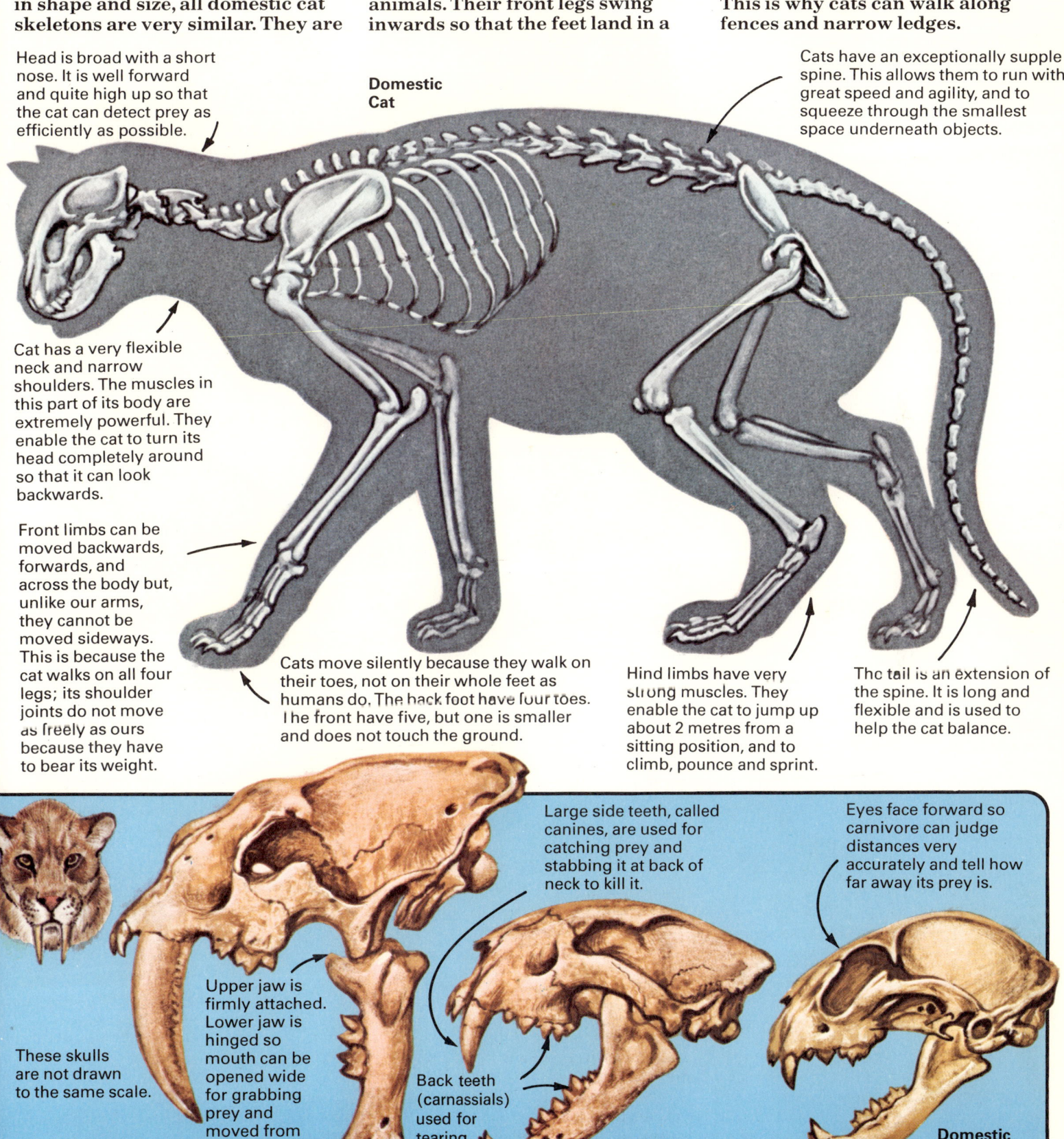

**Domestic Cat**

Head is broad with a short nose. It is well forward and quite high up so that the cat can detect prey as efficiently as possible.

Cat has a very flexible neck and narrow shoulders. The muscles in this part of its body are extremely powerful. They enable the cat to turn its head completely around so that it can look backwards.

Front limbs can be moved backwards, forwards, and across the body but, unlike our arms, they cannot be moved sideways. This is because the cat walks on all four legs; its shoulder joints do not move as freely as ours because they have to bear its weight.

Cats move silently because they walk on their toes, not on their whole feet as humans do. The back feet have four toes. The front have five, but one is smaller and does not touch the ground.

Cats have an exceptionally supple spine. This allows them to run with great speed and agility, and to squeeze through the smallest space underneath objects.

Hind limbs have very strong muscles. They enable the cat to jump up about 2 metres from a sitting position, and to climb, pounce and sprint.

The tail is an extension of the spine. It is long and flexible and is used to help the cat balance.

These skulls are not drawn to the same scale.

**Smilodon**

Upper jaw is firmly attached. Lower jaw is hinged so mouth can be opened wide for grabbing prey and moved from side to side for chewing.

Large side teeth, called canines, are used for catching prey and stabbing it at back of neck to kill it.

Back teeth (carnassials) used for tearing.

**Dinictis**

Eyes face forward so carnivore can judge distances very accurately and tell how far away its prey is.

**Domestic Cat**

# A cat's body

Cats spend much of their time asleep, but when they feel like it, they can move with lightning speed. They are among the top ten all-round athletes of the animal world. Cats have amazingly flexible bodies, but you may wonder how they manage to keep so fit when they take so little exercise. The answer lies largely in the lengthy stretching routine they go through on waking. This involves a whole series of leg, paw and back stretching movements, beginning with an upright thrust, that arches the cat's back.

The cat's body shape has developed for pouncing, springing, jumping, climbing and sprinting. Cats are perfectly equipped for fast, short runs but their heart and lungs are not built to cope with the "staying power" needed for longer runs.

Fur is the main feature that distinguishes one cat from another. All kittens have soft downy fur, but between four and six months old, the adult coat grows and noticeably changes their appearance. A cat's fur may be long or short, all one colour or a mixture of several.

Cats are very good at balancing on narrow ledges such as garden fences. Their powerful muscles, light bones and flexible joints make them very agile and their sharp claws help them to grip well.

The muscles of a cat's body must co-ordinate (work together), when it jumps from any height down to the ground. The positioning of the tail, head and limbs is specially important.

A cat can bend its spine almost double, enabling it to wash around the base of its tail. Notice how it twists its body to balance in this position with one leg in the air.

## Making paw prints

TUBE OF LINO-PRINTING INK (DARK COLOUR) — SHEET OF GLASS — ROLL INK ONTO GLASS — WHITE PAPER — INKED GLASS — FINISHED PRINT

You can make prints of cats' paws in the following way:

Spread a thin line of non-toxic printing ink on a sheet of glass, or other smooth surface. Roll out the ink on the glass with a printing roller, or spread it evenly with a brush. Put the glass on the floor surrounded by sheets of white paper. Place the cat gently on the inked surface. The cat will walk off the glass onto the paper (try bribing it with a bowl of food), leaving sets of paw prints.

Notice the difference between the back and front paws, and compare your cat's prints with those of other cats.

## Tongue, teeth, whiskers

A cat's tongue is long and thin, and extremely versatile. One moment it may be used for lapping milk, its edges curled up like a spoon, and the next it is being used for grooming the cat's fur.

If a cat licks your hand, you will notice how rough its tongue feels. The tongue's surface is covered with small, backward-pointing projections, called papillae, and these act like a comb when the cat licks its fur. Cats also use their tongues for tasting; they are sensitive to salt, sour and bitter tastes, and possibly to water.

Cats have long, sharp canine teeth, which are used for catching and killing prey. They are also used in grooming, to tease out

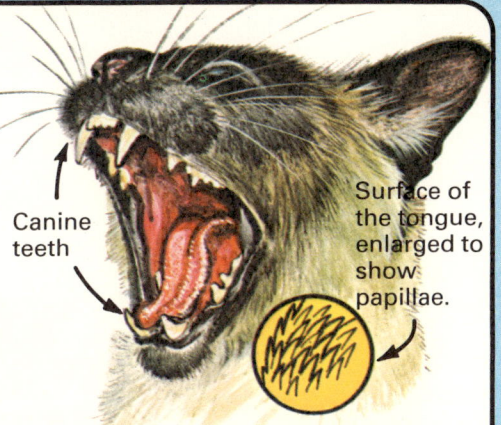

Canine teeth

Surface of the tongue, enlarged to show papillae.

knotted hair or dirt. Their back teeth are used for chewing. The front teeth, or incisors, are very small and are not used much. Old cats' incisors may drop out.

Cats' whiskers are very sensitive. They act as feelers and help the cat avoid obstacles.

## Fur

Base of a single hair, enlarged.
Skin
Hair
Hair muscle

Fur is a waterproof covering which protects the cat's body from bites and scratches, and from getting too hot or cold. Most cats have two kinds of hair, downy underhairs and coarse overhairs or guard hairs. The guard hairs are sensitive, like whiskers, and enable the cat to feel pain and pleasure.

Cats can use their fur to make themselves look larger and more threatening. Each guard hair has a muscle attached to it and when this tightens, the hair stands on end.

## Eyes

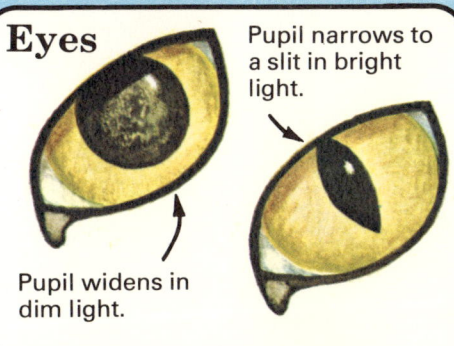

Pupil narrows to a slit in bright light.

Pupil widens in dim light.

Cats have excellent vision in daylight, but really unique vision at night when most of their hunting is done. Special tissue at the back of the eye enables them to use very dim light that is useless to humans.

## Ears

Ears turn to face direction of sound, and can move separately.

Cats can hear sounds that are higher-pitched and softer than the ones we can hear. Their ears can move faster than dogs' ears, and they can quickly pick up sounds from a particular direction. The ears also express feelings, such as aggression (see page 9).

## Tail

The long, flexible tail is an extension of the cat's spine. It is an important balancing aid and is held out behind when the cat jumps or springs. It can tell you a lot about a cat's mood (see page 9).

## Claws and paws

Claw withdrawn in sheathed position.

Claw extended ready for use.

Ligaments  Bone  Tendon

Rough surface of paw pads and claws both help cat grip when climbing.

Outer shell of claw drops off with wear, leaving sharp claw underneath.

Cats can learn to use their paws for scooping food out of tins.

Cats' paws are used for climbing, feeding, washing, digging, hunting and playing. The cushioned paw pads enable a cat to walk silently, land safely when jumping, and also to feel, as they are very sensitive.

Cats' sharp, curved claws do not get blunt because, unlike dogs' claws (which are always visible), they are kept sheathed when not in use. To extend the claws, muscles in the cat's leg contract. This tightens the tendons (cord-like bands of tissue) attached to these muscles. The tendons pull down the bones that bear the claws, exposing them.

# Cat language

Cats communicate with other cats, other animals and people by means of their own special language. This is made up of a range of sounds, facial expressions and movements, each of which has a precise meaning.

Some cats "talk" more than others, but most can make about 16 different sounds. The most important sounds are miaow, purr, hiss, mutter, growl and yowl. By watching carefully, you can quickly learn to understand what a cat is "saying" when it twitches its tail and mews, or flattens its ears and growls.

## The language of smell

Cats have glands, which produce scent, on each side of their forehead, and on their lips, chin and tail. They use scent to show friendship and "ownership." When a friendly cat rubs its head against your legs, it is marking you with scent from the glands on its head. Cats that are friendly will mark one another in the same way. Unlike the scent used to mark territory, we can't smell this.

Cats also mark out their territory by scratching trees with their front claws, and by rubbing against objects to leave scent from glands on their head.

Cats are very possessive about their home area, or territory. Toms (male cats) and some females mark out their territory regularly by spraying their urine against objects such as trees and shrubs. The urine contains a strong odour which indicates ownership of the area to other cats and warns them against intruding. The dots in the picture show the places which a tom might mark.

## Cat talk

Growling and hissing are used as threats, to warn other animals, and often other cats, to keep away. A cat may growl and hiss at a strange dog, even if the dog is friendly.

The familiar low, rumbling sound of a cat purring is a sign of contentment or pleasure. No-one is quite sure how this sound is made, but you can feel the vibrations if you touch a cat's throat on its voice-box, or put your hand on its chest.

A cat will miaow loudly when it wants something, such as food or to be let outside. This is an unmistakably demanding sound. Cats can express many different needs by varying the tone of their miaows.

A lazily contented cat will roll over onto its back and lie with its front limbs bent and its eyes half-closed. Exposing its belly is a sign of trust and security.

A cat will run to greet its owner with its tail held up like this.

A relaxed and happy cat will walk with its tail held high in the air, the tip just bending over slightly.

An inquisitive cat pricks its ears, listening for sounds. As it concentrates on the object of interest, its pupils widen and its whiskers lift and twitch.

## Body language

Cats express their feelings with their whole bodies, especially with their face and tail. They normally use body language more than sound when they are "talking" to one another. Sounds are used mainly when they are with people.

Watch a cat's face and see how its eyes vary from being half-closed with contentment to wide open with fear or surprise. Its ears may be laid back flat in anger or fear, or pricked in curiosity. Its tail may be held erect in friendship or lashing from side to side in anger. Notice that it is the precise combination of ear, eye, mouth and whisker movements used together with the body and tail movements that express the cat's feelings.

When annoyed or irritated, a cat stands stiff-legged, swishing its tail from side to side. The pupils of its eyes widen slightly.

If a cat is threatened by another cat it tries to make itself look as frightening as possible. It raises its fur and bushes out its tail to make itself look larger. It also flattens its ears, widens its pupils, extends its claws and draws back its lips, revealing its teeth.

A frightened cat, cornered by a dog, will crouch with its back arched. Its whiskers and ears will be held back and it may raise a paw, ready to defend itself.

When two friendly cats meet, they greet each other by touching whiskers and noses, sniffing the areas where there are scent glands.

# Hunting

All members of the cat family are carnivores (meat-eating animals). Their structure and behaviour have developed over thousands of years to make them almost perfect hunters. They are able to stalk their prey silently, creeping forward on their padded feet, and then pounce on the unsuspecting victim using their sharp claws and teeth for seizing and killing it.

The ability to hunt is instinctive or natural to all cats. Even domestic cats, which do not need to live by hunting prey, have the same instincts. Cats' skill at hunting is made possible by their well-developed sight and hearing. (Dogs, on the other hand, rely more on the sense of smell).

The simple tests on this page show that if you imitate the sound and movement of a cat's prey, the cat will begin stalking the "prey," even though it is only make-believe.

Kittens start play-hunting when they are about six weeks old, stalking and pouncing on one another. But they learn to kill and eat prey by experience, usually by watching their mother.

## Stalking and killing

**1** When a cat spots a small animal, such as a mouse, it will freeze in a crouched position close to the ground, with its tail tip twitching in excitement. It watches the prey carefully to get an idea of its speed and to see in which direction it is moving.

### Learning to hunt

Kittens love to stalk and ambush one another. They will chase and pounce on anything that moves, even dead leaves blown by the wind. It is through these games that kittens develop hunting skills.

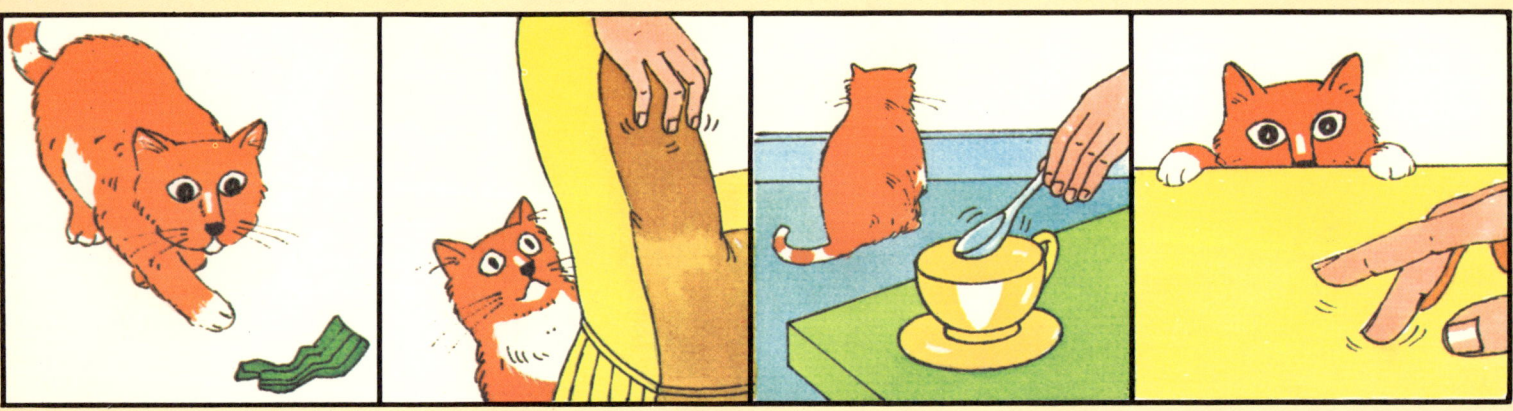

Cats are attracted to rustling and scratching noises which sound like small animals scurrying about in dead leaves or long grass. Swift movement also attracts a cat's attention.

Try to find out which noises and movements attract your cat, and watch it stalking the "prey." Crinkle up a small piece of paper or silver foil and toss it on the floor. Scratch your finger nails on carpet or chair covers. Tap a spoon on a cup. Tip-toe your fingers across the top of a table. Notice that the cat may look up when you tap the cup but it will not start to stalk.

**2** Having studied its prey, the cat then begins its attack. It moves forward quickly in a low stalking run, with its tail swishing gently.

**3** As the cat nears the prey, it prepares to pounce. Its hind legs push back and its bottom is raised up and begins to sway from side to side, while its tail twitches more wildly.

**4** The cat springs forward, reaching out with its front paws to pin down the prey. As it seizes the prey, the cat spreads its hind legs further apart to act as a brake.

**5** Grasping the prey with its sharp claws, the cat is able to make a quick kill by sinking its front teeth into the back of the animal's neck.

### Prey

Rats, mice and other small rodents are a cat's usual prey. Cats also stalk birds and frogs, and insects such as flies and butterflies.

Cats do not often succeed in catching birds because they always follow the same pattern of movements in stalking prey. By the time the cat is ready to pounce, the bird will be flying away. Cats may also try to catch goldfish, but usually grow bored before they succeed.

When stalking prey, a cat keeps its body low to the ground and moves swiftly and silently in a set pattern of movements. Its spongy, roughened paw pads with tufts of fur between them enable it to walk quietly on any surface. The cat tries to attack its prey from above and behind so that the prey is taken by surprise.

# How cats behave

Cats spend most of their time grooming and washing, or sleeping. They are extremely particular about keeping clean and always wash after a meal and when they wake up. In grooming, they use their tongues to "comb" their fur, and their teeth to tease out any knotted hair or dirt. Grooming also often expresses a cat's feelings. It may be a sign of friendship, embarrassment or aloofness.

Cats show a natural curiosity and will investigate any object they find lying around. Often such objects make good playthings, especially if the cat can dive inside or if the object is small enough to be moved around.

Play is particularly important in the first few weeks of a cat's life. It is largely through playing that kittens learn how to hunt for food, and how to escape from enemies and defend themselves.

Cats are friendly, peace-loving animals and will usually run away from an enemy rather than become involved in a fight. But cats, especially tomcats, are possessive about their own territory. They will become very aggressive towards intruders.

**1 Curiosity** Try this test to see how inquisitive your cat is. Put a large paper bag on the floor where the cat can see it.

**2** The cat will first inspect the bag from a distance. It will then walk up to it, sniff around and peep inside.

**3** It may also pat the bag to see if it moves. Finally, it may dive inside and turn round to peer out at you.

**Sleeping**

Much of a cat's sleep is a very light sleep, called a cat nap, from which the cat can wake instantly. Cats will nap in odd places, often perched on ledges.

Cats sleep soundly only when they feel secure, in their own box or on a favourite chair. During this deep sleep, cats may dream. Their limbs and faces twitch and they may make little muttering noises.

**1 Grooming and washing**
A cat can twist its head right round over its shoulder to wash and groom the side of its body.

**2** Cats use their forepaws to wash their faces and ears. First, they lick the paw well to moisten it.

The damp paw is then wiped across the cat's face in a sweeping movement from the ear down to the chin.

# Aggression

A tomcat will defend its own garden or territory against dogs or other cats, unless they are friends. It will warn off intruders by standing with its tail held up stiffly, and its fur ruffled to make it look larger and more threatening. It may also arch its back and hiss or spit.

Kittens and young cats learn self-defence through play-fighting. They roll on their backs, kicking with their hind feet and trying to clasp each other's necks.

When adult cats fight, they do not usually roll over and expose the belly, which is a sign of giving in. Instead, the loser will turn and walk away. Tomcats may fight to defend their territory or when competing for a mate.

When faced with a larger, unfriendly animal, such as a strange dog, a cat will flee rather than fight. It may escape up the nearest tree. If the cat is cornered and cannot escape, it will become aggressive and prepare to strike out at the dog.

**3** Cats groom each other to show affection. They like to be stroked, a form of grooming, by their owners.

**4** Cats do not groom themselves just to keep clean. If a cat finds itself in a difficult situation and it feels embarrassed, anxious or annoyed, it may automatically start to wash. Scientists call this sort of behaviour "displacement activity." The picture shows how a cat that is walking may stop to groom itself when embarrassed. If a cat is sitting, it may give long licks down over one shoulder. People behave in a similar way. In awkward situations, they scratch their heads or fiddle with clothing.

# Intelligence and learning

Cats have exceptional abilities and highly developed senses which, in the past, led people to believe that they had magical powers. Even now, many people still believe that cats have a "sixth sense." However, research by scientists shows that it is the exceptionally acute senses and high level of intelligence that enables cats to perform apparently amazing feats.

### Three kinds of behaviour
Cats show three different kinds of behaviour. The simplest of these is involuntary or reflex behaviour, such as flicking an ear when the hairs around it are touched. People show these reflex actions too. If you touch something very hot, for example, you automatically let it go before you feel pain.

### Instincts
The second kind of behaviour is instinctive. Most of a kitten's early activities are instinctive responses to its environment. For example, newborn kittens instinctively react to the smell of milk and suckle from their mother, and a litter of kittens instinctively huddles together for warmth when their mother leaves the nest.

### Learning and memory
The third kind of behaviour is the result of experience. A cat learns by imitating its mother, other cats or even humans, and also by trial and error. As kittens grow up, more of their behaviour is guided by learning and memory, but basic instincts are still important.

### Opening windows

Cats are lovers of freedom and dislike being shut up in enclosed spaces. Many learn to open windows and doors so that they can come and go as they please.

**1** When a cat falls upside down from a height, it immediately starts to right itself.

**2** First the head twists on the neck.

**3** Then the chest follows so that the front paws face the ground.

**4** Next the spine twists so that the back legs face the ground.

**5** This brings the legs into position for landing.

# Falling

Cats have a remarkable sense of balance and more flexible bodies than dogs. If a cat falls upside down from a height, it will twist its head and body in an orderly series of movements so that it lands safely on its feet. This is a reflex action, called the righting reflex.

**REMEMBER! CATS ARE VERY INDEPENDENT AND DO NOT LIKE BEING HANDLED ROUGHLY OR BEING DROPPED. THEY HAVE GOOD MEMORIES AND BECOME WARY OF ANYONE WHO MISTREATS THEM.**

# Homing ability

Cats are able to find their way back to their own home territory even when they are some distance away from home, as when their owners move house and take them to live in a new area. Some cats have been known to travel hundreds of kilometres to return home. They may be able to tell which direction to travel from the position of the sun in the sky.

Usually, cats can only find their way home over much shorter distances. The actual distance is thought to depend on the cat's ability to recognize its surroundings. City cats have small territories and are not used to wandering far. They can only find their way home from about one to two kilometres away. Country cats nearly always have larger territories and can get home from distances of up to 16 kilometres.

# Time sense

Cats have a very strong sense of time. Wild members of the cat family learn the movements of animals around them and the best time of day to go hunting. Similarly, domestic cats learn to fit their daily habits into their owner's routine and know when to expect food. Some cats learn their owner's routine so well that they will wake them a few minutes before the alarm clock rings in the morning.

# Recognizing familiar sounds

Many cats are able to detect their owner's arrival long before anyone else is aware that the person is near. This is because they have excellent hearing and can learn to distinguish their owner's footsteps from all others. Some cats also learn to recognize the sound of their owner's car engine.

Because they are intelligent, cats quickly learn how to get the things they want. A cat that accidentally knocks over a milk jug will drink the milk that spills out. When the cat next sees a jug it may deliberately knock it over. The cat has learned that the jug is a likely source of food. This is one reason why cats should never be allowed onto tables.

# Watching cats

Cats eat some kinds of grass, perhaps as a kind of medicine. When they wash, cats swallow some of their fur and this can collect in balls in their stomach. To get rid of these fur balls they eat grass, which makes them sick.

Some cats will eat wool if they are very bored. They start to behave like kittens, kneading with their front paws and sucking at something woollen, such as their own blanket or a pullover. They do this because they want attention and company.

Cats can be jealous of other cats in their own home. If a cat thinks it is getting less than its fair share of attention, it may push in when another is being stroked. It may also try to get attention by rubbing against its owner's legs.

Some cats appear to enjoy watching television with their owners. It is probably the flickering movement of the screen which fascinates them.

Cats sometimes seem to admire themselves in mirrors. They are attracted by the movement they can see. Some cats may even try to look behind a mirror to find the "other cat" they think they have seen.

Most cats do not like getting wet. They seem to have a natural fear of water although they can swim well. But some cats are fascinated by the movement of water and will sit watching a tap drip. Some may even paw at a trickle of water.

Cats are amazingly patient. They will spend their time crouching by a mousehole if they can smell mice. This is because cats hunt prey by ambushing it, and learn to wait for the right time to pounce.

Cats that go hunting at night often bring home prey and present it to their owner. This is not done just to "show off." It is based on the natural instinct of a mother cat bringing home prey to her kittens for food.

Cats can be very aloof. By nature, they are independent animals and please only themselves. Sometimes, a cat may not want to play when you do. It will ignore you and may start washing.

## Keeping a record

It is fun to keep a scrap book if you have your own cat. You can make drawings of your cat as it grows up, and take photographs if you have a camera. You may find bits of fur and claws and discarded whiskers you can stick in your book. Make notes about your cat's behaviour, using this book to help you.

## The ageing cat

Nose may become dry and slightly scaly.

Cat eats less because it is being less active and its sense of taste and smell are not so good. Teeth and gums often look less healthy. Gums may recede to show base of teeth. Front teeth (incisors) often become loose and fall out.

Eyes may become paler in colour and look dull. They may sometimes get watery.

Coat loses its glossy shine and hair may fall out more than usual. Cat may find it difficult to groom itself because of stiffening joints, and so will need to be brushed more.

Young cats have a triangular-shaped face, broad across the forehead with narrow cheeks.

As a cat (especially a tom) gets older, its cheeks fill out. The triangular shape of its face has turned upside down.

Some elderly cats look thinner. The sides of their body sink inwards as the muscles lose their firmness.

Cats live longer than most other pets, and usually slightly longer than dogs. A cat's average lifespan is about 12 to 15 years, but some cats have lived 30 years. Cats are normally active until they are about 10 or 12 years old. After this, they become less alert. Their sense of balance may not be so good and they move about more slowly. Older cats need to be kept warm. They should be given several small meals a day rather than one or two larger ones and should not be allowed to get too fat. They may want to go outside more often to urinate. These changes are all due to their bodies working less efficiently as they get older.

17

# Courtship and mating

Healthy female kittens can mate and produce kittens of their own when they are only six to eight months old and not yet fully grown. Males take slightly longer to develop. They are usually between nine and fifteen months old when they are first able to mate.

Cats do not usually mate during the shortest days of the year. When the days are longer, in the period from spring to autumn, females have a two to three week pattern or cycle of activity which is repeated continuously. For the first week or so of the cycle, the female is able to mate and is said to be "on heat" or "in season." If she is not mated during this time, a resting phase follows, until the next period of heat about two weeks later.

Females on heat are often courted by several toms if they are allowed to roam freely. A female will mate several times in one heat period, so she may mate with more than one of the toms that court her. She rests for up to an hour between each mating and will strike any tom that approaches before she is ready.

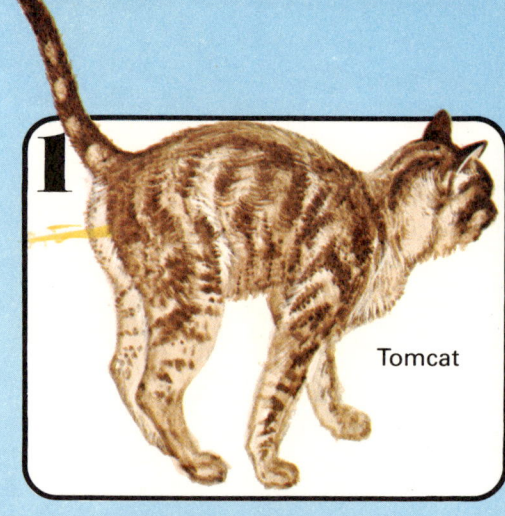

Some toms will court and mate only in their own territory, which they mark out by spraying with their urine (see page 8). When a tom finds a female on heat, his first move is to spray the area with urine.

Female rejects tom by growling and striking at him with her claws out.

When a female is on heat, she calls to attract toms to her and gives off a smell which they find very attractive. For two to three days, the toms court her, but she is not ready to mate and will reject advances made by any of them. This is a safeguard from the wild, to give the males plenty of time to find the female before she goes off heat.

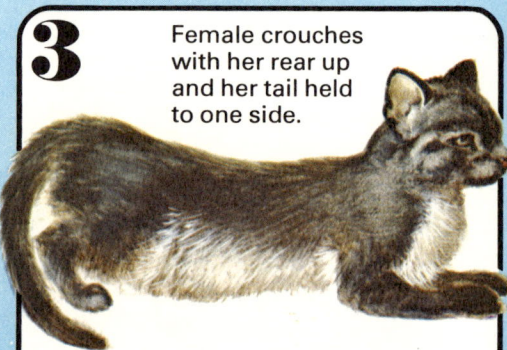

Female crouches with her rear up and her tail held to one side.

When she is ready to mate, the female's mood changes. She begins to roll and rubs her head against anything nearby. She then crouches low, making treading movements with her hind legs and purring.

Tomcat grasps female by scruff of neck.

When he sees that the female is ready, the tom approaches her sideways from behind. He mounts her, grasping the scruff of her neck with his teeth and gripping her body between his front legs.

The female remains still while the tom thrusts his penis into her, releasing his sperm. After a few seconds, she lets out a piercing cry and pulls away from him by twisting sideways.

Immediately after mating, the female rolls over and over and licks herself frantically. If the tom tries to approach again at this time, the female will growl and strike out at him.

## How an unborn kitten grows

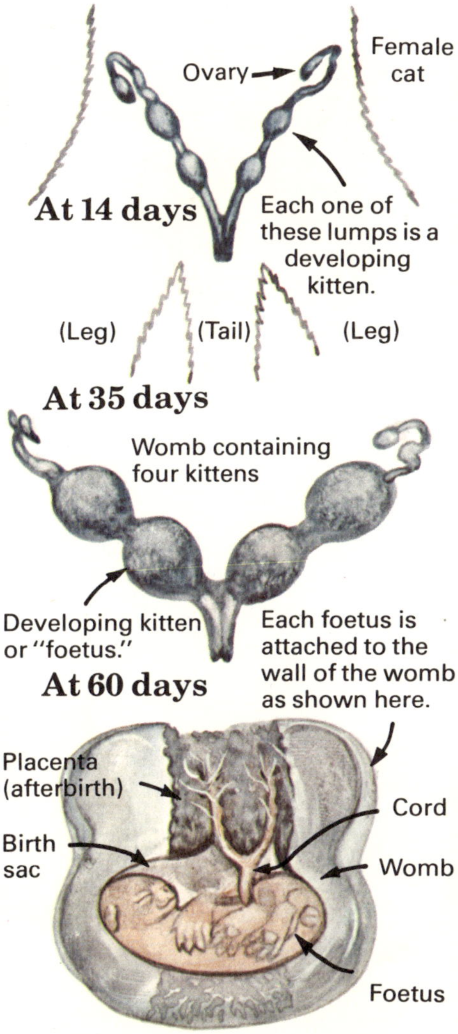

**At 14 days** — Ovary, Female cat. Each one of these lumps is a developing kitten.

(Leg) (Tail) (Leg)

**At 35 days** — Womb containing four kittens. Developing kitten or "foetus." Each foetus is attached to the wall of the womb as shown here.

**At 60 days** — Placenta (afterbirth), Birth sac, Cord, Womb, Foetus.

Eggs from the ovary combine with sperm from the tom and start to develop into kittens in the female's womb. Kittens are born about 65 days after mating.

Noisy fights take place between toms when they gather around a female on heat. The strongest will win the right to mate with her.

## Sexing kittens

Female — Male (about 4 weeks old)

To tell whether a kitten is male or female, lift up its tail and look closely at its rear. If the two small back openings are about twelve millimetres apart, the kitten is a male. If they are very close together and appear to meet, the kitten is a female.

There are usually one to four kittens in a litter, but there can be up to eight. The more kittens there are, the smaller they will be. It is quite difficult to tell male and female kittens apart.

## Fighting toms

If you get a male kitten as a pet, it is wise to have its sex organs removed by a vet at about four to five months old. This is called "neutering". It will prevent the kitten from developing a tom's habits of spraying urine, fighting and straying.

## How many kittens?

FEMALE CAT = ONE LITTER (4 KITTENS AVERAGE)

+ AT 3 YEARS
+ AT 5 YEARS
+ AT 7 YEARS
+ AT 9 YEARS
+ AT 11 YEARS
= 100 KITTENS

A female cat is able to mate again within a few weeks of giving birth. She can produce as many as 100 kittens during her life as this chart shows. If you get a female kitten as a pet, it may be best to have her sex organs removed by a vet so she cannot have kittens. This is called "spaying."

# The birth of kittens

During the last week of her pregnancy, a female cat becomes less active. Her stomach is very large and her nipples are pink and swollen. Cats are naturally excellent mothers. They rarely need help with the birth of their kittens unless there are any complications. The kittens are usually born not more than one hour apart, and a whole litter may be produced in less than an hour.

After the birth of the last kitten, the mother cleans her hindquarters and then curls herself round on her side so that she encircles and protects the kittens while they suckle. As long as she continues to feed the kittens, the mother is likely to lose weight even though she will eat more. She should be given two or three times as much food as normal.

The first three weeks of a kitten's life are roughly equal to the first 18 months of a human baby's life. The kittens do not venture out of the nest until they start to walk at about three weeks old. They may pat one another and begin to play by the end of the third week.

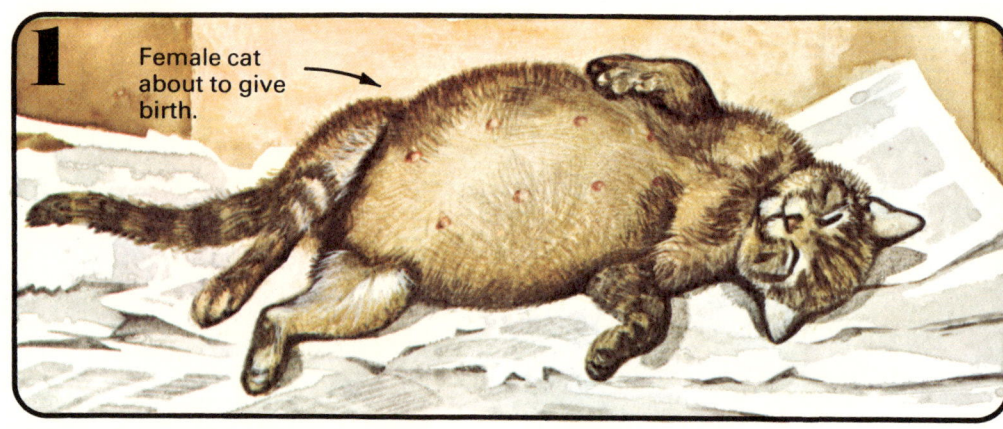

**1** Female cat about to give birth.

**If your cat is going to have kittens, you should provide her with a strong cardboard box lined with clean newspaper. The box should be put in a warm, quiet, draught-free** place where the cat will not be disturbed. When she is about to give birth, the cat will become restless and she may begin shredding the paper in her box to make a nest.

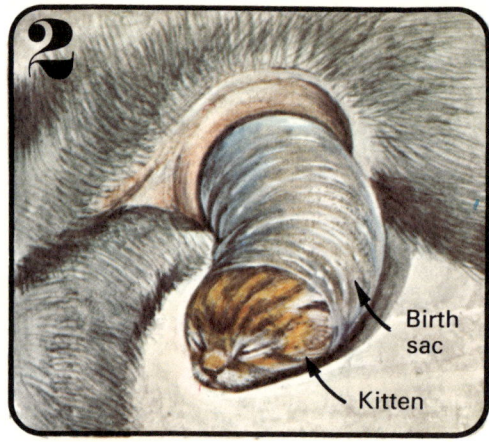

**2** Birth sac. Kitten.

**Each kitten is born in a thin, transparent bag or sac. This sac breaks either at birth or just before, releasing the fluid inside it.**

**3** Newborn kitten.

**The mother cat bites the cord, licks the newly born kitten vigorously to get it breathing and to dry it, then eats the afterbirth.**

**4** Kitten suckles from mother's teat. Hold kitten in one hand like this. Newborn kittens must be fed every two hours. Control milk flow by holding finger over open end of bottle.

**As soon as a kitten has been dried, it searches for a teat to suckle from. Kittens are born blind, so they find their mother's teats by smell and touch.**

**If a cat has more than four kittens, she may not be able to feed them all. You can feed young kittens using a special feeding bottle like this. A cat's milk is much richer than cow's** milk, so ask your vet how to make up a substitute feed. If a kitten is fed on cow's milk alone, it will starve to death. The vet will also tell you how often to feed kittens as they get older.

## 5 One week old

The mother washes each kitten, especially around its head and tail. Washing around its tail makes the kitten excrete. The mother eats the urine and solid waste to keep the nest clean.

By the time the kittens are a week old, each one in the litter will have "claimed" a teat as its own. It will now feed only from this teat.

For the first one or two days after birth, the mother stays with her kittens continuously. After they are about a week old, she will leave them for several hours at a time. The kittens keep warm when she is away by sleeping in a heap, but as soon as she comes back they nuzzle up to her and start feeding. The kittens can only crawl along on their stomachs at this stage and spend most of their time suckling and sleeping. They grow quickly and double their weight in the first nine days.

Kitten is born blind. Its eyes stay closed for about nine days.

Kitten's claws are not yet retractable.

Kitten has no teeth for the first two weeks.

If a kitten gets separated from its mother it lets out a shrill wailing sound which enables its mother to find it.

## 6 Nine days old

Eyes just opening.

At about nine days old, the kittens' eyes open. All kittens' eyes are a milky blue colour when they first open. It is a few days before the kitten can see properly.

## 7 Three weeks old

By three weeks old, the kittens can stand quite well and they take their first steps. Hearing improves and their baby or "milk" teeth are beginning to appear.

If a mother cat senses danger she will carry her kittens to safety. She picks each one up in her mouth by the scruff of its neck. The kitten curls up into a ball to protect itself.

# Growing up

Between four to eight weeks is a very important time in a kitten's life. The experiences it has at this age shape its development as an adult, so it should have plenty of contact with people during this period.

At three to four weeks, the mother leaves the kittens on their own for longer, but she is still very protective towards them. Kittens begin to eat some solid food at about four weeks, so they take less milk. (This process is called "weaning"). By the time they are six to eight weeks old, kittens are quite independent.

**A mother's ability to produce milk depends on the kittens continuing to suckle. Kittens develop a kneading action with their forepaws to encourage the flow of milk.**

**As kittens grow stronger they play more vigorously. They tire easily at this stage and fall asleep in a pile so that they keep each other warm.**

## Coming out of the nest

The mother continues to groom her kittens until they are about seven weeks old. As they grow up, they often respond by licking her face and neck.

Kittens paw at each other's faces and bodies when they first start to play together. Playing is very important, as it helps them to develop skills they will need as adults.

Kittens' sense of smell is well developed. They sniff at everything around them.

**By four weeks old, the kittens are exploring their surroundings thoroughly. They will have most of their milk teeth and will bite and chew everything they find. As they spend more time out of the nest, they will start to excrete away from it. It is useful to keep a bucket of water and sponge handy for mopping up.**

Kittens use their paws to investigate things that interest them. They hook objects towards them for closer inspection. By four weeks their claws have become retractable.

# Weaning

**1**

When kittens leave the nest, they will see their mother eating from a bowl, and may try imitating her. You can begin weaning kittens now with baby food or dried milk, made up as indicated on the packet.

**2**

Kittens should be introduced to solid food, such as finely minced raw meat, in the fourth week when they have most of their milk teeth. They should have learned to lap and chew, and be fully weaned by the time they are six weeks old.

Cat litter or earth in tray.

When it moves from the nest a kitten may imitate its mother and use a toilet tray. If it is slow to learn, you can help by placing it on a tray regularly after meals.

## 1 Learning from mother

By the time they are six weeks old, kittens have become very adventurous and will play with almost anything. The mother cat is very tolerant and will allow them to play with her tail, twitching it invitingly to and fro. The kittens start to learn hunting skills by stalking and pouncing on her tail.

**2**

The mother cat actively encourages her kittens to play, but if they become too rough or misbehave, she will bat them with her paw.

**3**

Kittens have to be taught to recognize danger. They have little sense of fear and must learn from their mother which animals are friends or enemies.

**4**

Kittens learn how to groom and wash themselves by watching and imitating their mother. They often groom one another.

## Handling kittens

Mother will watch anxiously when you pick up a kitten.

From six weeks old, kittens should be handled frequently so that they get used to being picked up and will not scratch and bite. Always pick up a kitten or cat with one hand underneath to support it.

# A new pet

Many people find kittens irresistible and are tempted to buy one on impulse. But a kitten soon grows into a cat and most cats live to at least ten years of age. Although cats are very independent animals, they need affection and companionship, so do not get one if you are likely to be away from home a lot.

There are many lovely breeds of cats (see pages 30 and 31), but most people prefer a mongrel (a cross-bred cat). Pure bred cats cost a lot of money and are usually kept by people for entering in shows.

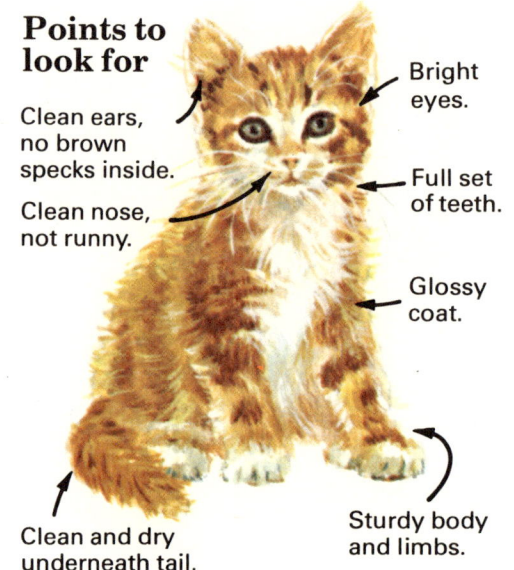

**Points to look for**
- Clean ears, no brown specks inside.
- Clean nose, not runny.
- Bright eyes.
- Full set of teeth.
- Glossy coat.
- Clean and dry underneath tail.
- Sturdy body and limbs.

You can buy kittens from pet shops, but if possible, buy one from the house where it has been born so that you can see that the mother cat is alert, healthy and well cared for.

Kittens should not be taken from their mother until they are fully weaned at about seven or eight weeks. When you go to collect your kitten take a cat-carrying basket with you. Ask whether the kitten has been vaccinated against feline infectious enteritis. If not, you should take it to a vet straight away as this disease can kill cats.

Cardboard or wooden box with hole cut in one side makes a good bed. Line with newspaper and an old rug. If very cold, add a hot-water bottle (hand-hot water) wrapped in a blanket.

Plastic tray with sides about 8 cm high. Half-fill with cat litter and place on newspaper in a quiet corner. Change litter frequently.

If your kitten is likely to spend a lot of time outside when older, you should get it used to wearing a collar with an address tag. The collar should have an elastic insert so that the cat will not get strangled if caught while climbing a tree.

Elastic

Fresh water

Kitten should start with four small meals of varied food a day.

Cotton reel

Ball of silver paper.

Ping-pong ball

Bell tied onto twig.

Kitten can be kept amused with simple toys such as these.

Before you take a new kitten home, you should get a few things ready. The most essential is a warm bed. A cardboard or wooden box is best, with newspaper and an old rug for bedding. Put the box in a corner away from draughts and where there is not too much noise.

The kitten should have fresh water available at all times and a litter tray. Even if you have a garden and plan to let the kitten excrete outside, you should provide it with a litter tray for a few weeks, until it knows you and is used to its new home.

Keep the kitten in one room to start with and gradually introduce it to the rest of the home over the next few days. Let it run around and explore its surroundings, and do not handle it too much at first. The breeder or pet shop will give you instructions for feeding.

## 1 Training

Cat flap

If you have a garden, you can train your kitten to ask to go outside to excrete. A cat flap fitted in the door allows a cat to come and go as it pleases.

## 2

Cats can be trained to claw at special scratching posts rather than at furniture. Hold the cat up to the post and move its paws up and down. You can buy posts at pet shops.

## 3

DON'T ALLOW KITTEN ON WORK SURFACES. IT IS UNHYGIENIC.

DON'T ALLOW KITTEN NEAR ELECTRIC FLEXES. IT MIGHT GET A SHOCK IF IT CHEWS A PLUGGED-IN FLEX.

DON'T ALLOW KITTEN ON TOP OF COOKER OR HIGH LEVEL GRILL. KITTENS LOVE WARMTH BUT THEY COULD EASILY BURN THEMSELVES.

Kittens are very inquisitive, so care must be taken to keep them away from dangers in the home, especially in the kitchen.

Do not allow a kitten to play near anyone who is cooking, in case they trip over it. Always guard fireplaces and electric fires.

## Exercise

You should play with your kitten as often as possible to exercise it and prevent it from becoming bored. All kittens love to chase and pounce on small objects tied to string.

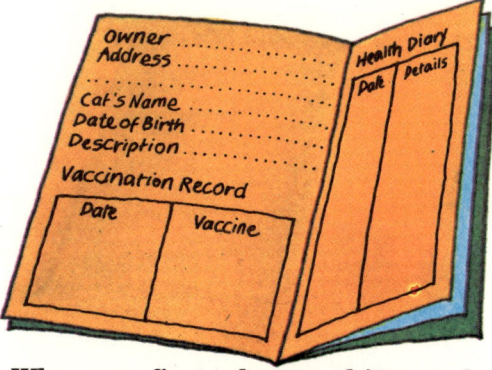

When you first take your kitten to be vaccinated, the vet will give you a certificate which shows when booster jabs will be needed. The certificate may be like this one, with space for notes about your cat's health. Make your own record book if you are not given one.

## Make a catnip mouse

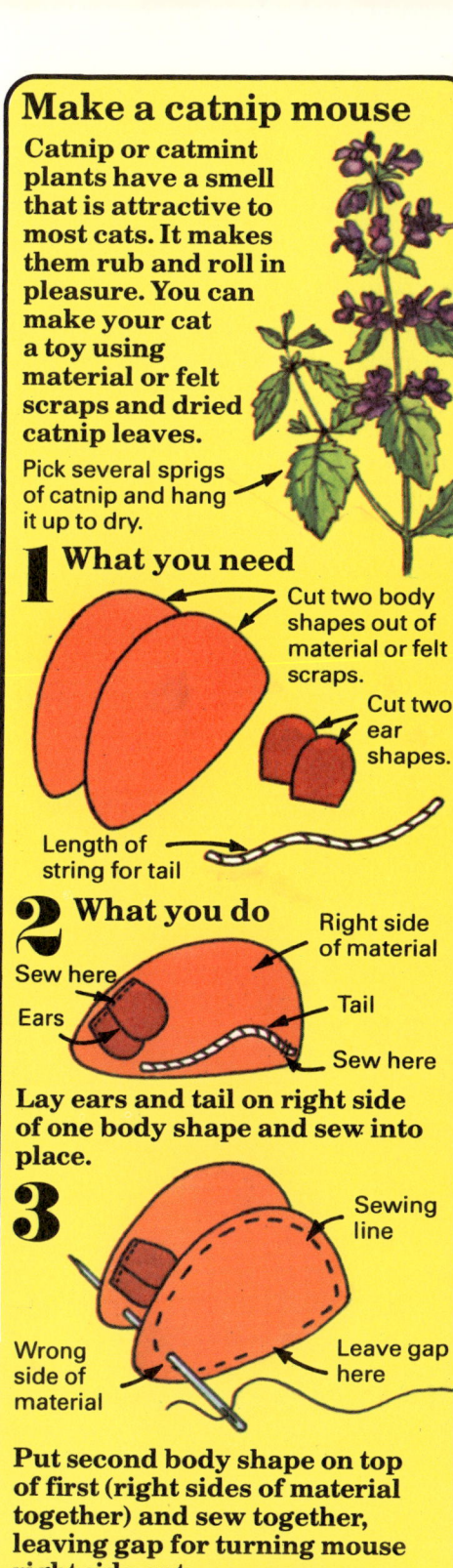

Catnip or catmint plants have a smell that is attractive to most cats. It makes them rub and roll in pleasure. You can make your cat a toy using material or felt scraps and dried catnip leaves.

Pick several sprigs of catnip and hang it up to dry.

### 1 What you need

Cut two body shapes out of material or felt scraps.
Cut two ear shapes.
Length of string for tail.

### 2 What you do

Right side of material
Sew here
Ears
Tail
Sew here

Lay ears and tail on right side of one body shape and sew into place.

### 3

Sewing line
Wrong side of material
Leave gap here

Put second body shape on top of first (right sides of material together) and sew together, leaving gap for turning mouse right side out.

### 4

Eye

Turn mouse right side out. Stuff with dried catnip and sew up hole in body. Draw on eyes with a marking pen.

# Looking after your cat

Cats make excellent pets. They are very easy to look after, as they do not need long walks or much training. A cat's main requirements for a healthy and happy life are the correct diet, cleanliness, warmth and human company. Feeding time is the high spot in a cat's day, so feed your cat at the same time each day as far as possible. Feed food at room temperature and do not leave uneaten food lying around.

From the time it is weaned, a kitten should be encouraged to eat a variety of foods. Cats can be very fussy eaters and if allowed to develop preferences may not eat a balanced diet. Adult cats need only one meal a day, but many people prefer to feed two slightly smaller meals. An adult male cat should weigh about 4½ kilograms and a female about 3 kilograms. Weigh your cat occasionally to make sure you are not overfeeding it.

Cats are very healthy animals. They do not need an annual check-up, but if you have any worries about your cat's health, do take it to a vet. Beware of taking in stray cats as they are often unhealthy and may have roundworms or tapeworms.

Cats can be fed raw foods, such as meat and offal, table scraps, fish, canned food, dried food or semi-dry food. Some also enjoy fresh milk but this may cause diarrhoea. Canned food is probably the best. It contains about 70 per cent water.

If you feed your cat dried food, you must make sure that it also has plenty of milk or water. A good idea is to mix the dried food with warm water. Eaten in large amounts, it can cause cats, especially neutered toms, severe problems in passing urine.

Mice are an ideal food for a cat. The circle shows what a mouse is made up of. It also contains vitamins in its liver.

## Fleas and ear mites

Fleas and ear mites are two problems often suffered by cats. Mites can damage hearing if left untreated, so go to a vet for ear drops if you suspect them. Fleas live in cats' fur and are difficult to see as they are very small. Brown specks in the fur may be flea droppings. Try the test shown here and if necessary treat your cat with flea powder. Follow the directions on the tin.

## Worms

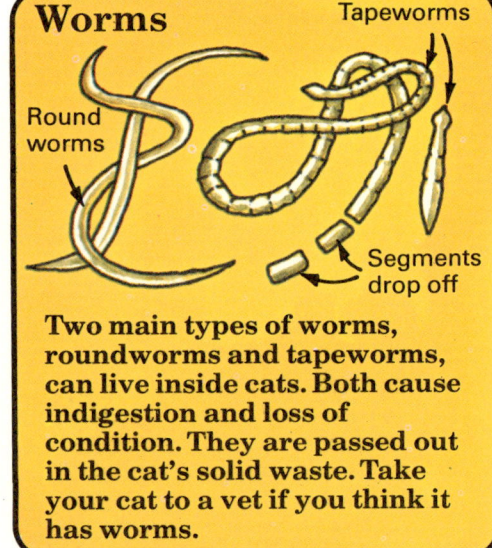

Two main types of worms, roundworms and tapeworms, can live inside cats. Both cause indigestion and loss of condition. They are passed out in the cat's solid waste. Take your cat to a vet if you think it has worms.

# Grooming

Use a bristle brush to groom your cat.

As soon as you get a kitten you should establish a grooming routine. Short-haired cats should be groomed once a week but long-haired ones need daily brushing. Any badly matted fur must be gently cut off.

# Travel

If you have to take your cat on journeys or to the vet, it is advisable to carry it in a special basket with a secure fastening. Line the bottom of the basket with paper to keep out draughts.

# Illness and injury

The most common sign of illness in cats is loss of appetite combined with vomiting. Never attempt to treat a cat yourself, always go to a vet.

If your cat is ill with a temperature or vomiting, wrap it up warmly and put it in a darkened room. A sick cat may bite, so handle it as little as possible. Call the vet.

If a cat gets run over, lay it on newspaper in a cardboard box, cover to keep warm and take it to a vet immediately.

# Holidays

If you go away, whether for a weekend or a long holiday, you must arrange for your cat to be looked after. Either ask a reliable neighbour to come in and feed the cat at its normal meal times or, for longer holidays, find recognized cat boarding kennels. Always go and look at kennels before you book to make sure they are clean and well equipped and that any cats there are being well cared for. You will need to book well in advance, especially in the summer.

DO'S AND DON'TS

DON'T LET A CAT EAT FROM DISHES THAT YOU USE YOURSELF. IT MAY BE CARRYING GERMS IN ITS MOUTH.

DON'T HANDLE A CAT TOO MUCH OR KISS OR NUZZLE IT. IT MAY SCRATCH YOU IF IT IS FEELING FED UP.

DON'T LET A CAT SLEEP ON YOUR BED. IT MAY HAVE FLEAS.

DON'T PUT A CAT OUT AT NIGHT. IT MAY CHOOSE TO GO OUT IF IT HAS A CAT FLAP, BUT DON'T FORCE IT TO.

DO WASH A CAT'S DISHES SEPARATELY, USING HOT SOAPY WATER. WASH THEM IMMEDIATELY AFTER EACH MEAL.

DO WASH YOUR HANDS AFTER HANDLING A CAT. CATS ARE VERY CLEAN ANIMALS BUT THEY CAN CARRY GERMS.

DO PROVIDE A CAT WITH ITS OWN BED AND PUT IT IN A WARM PLACE AWAY FROM DRAUGHTS.

# Kinds of cats

Domestic cats are divided into groups based on features such as shape of head and fur length. The grouping and naming of cats differs slightly in different countries but two main groups, longhair and shorthair cats, are recognized everywhere. Shorthair cats are divided into two groups: British or American and Foreign shorthairs.

Groups, or breeds, of cats are divided even further according to the colour and pattern of their coats and their eye colour. For example, the tabby is a British shorthair with distinctive coat markings. There are three kinds, or varieties, of tabby: brown, red and silver.

**Words used for describing cats**
**Cobby:** sturdily built body.
**Ear tufts:** tufts of hair at base of ears.
**Mask:** the face.
**Persian:** any longhair cat.
**Points:** feet, legs, ears, tail and mask. Most commonly used in describing Siamese cats, which have points of a different colour from main coat colour.
**Ruff:** the fur around the neck.
**Self:** a cat whose coat is the same colour all over, with no markings.
**Ticked:** hairs whose tips are a different colour from the rest of the hair.
**Whisker pads:** muscular pads from which the whiskers sprout.

### Foreign shorthair

Seal-pointed Siamese

Foreign shorthairs have short coats and are slim and dainty. They have long, wedge-shaped heads, large, pointed ears and slanting eyes.

### British or American shorthair

Brown tabby

British or American shorthairs have medium length coats and stocky bodies. They have broad heads with fairly short ears and noses.

### Longhair

Blue persian

Longhaired cats have long, glossy fur and cobby bodies. They have short legs and a broad head with small ears and a very short nose.

### Semi-longhair

Birman

Semi-longhaired cats are grouped with longhaired cats but they have a shorter coat. There are two varieties, Birman and Turkish.

## Breeding

From time to time, cats give birth to kittens that differ slightly in appearance from all the existing varieties of cats. If such a kitten is admired, it will be carefully selected and bred with another similar-looking cat. In this way, a new variety of cat gradually emerges. All the many different kinds of pedigree, or pure bred, cats that exist today are the result of this selective kind of breeding.

A pedigree cat is one whose family tree is known for at least five generations. Its pedigree must be officially registered.

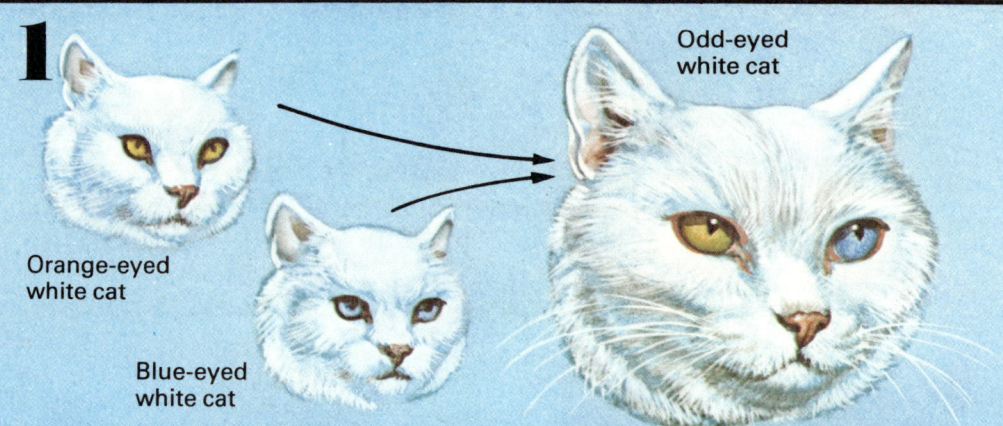

White cats with blue eyes tend to be deaf. To correct this fault, breeders sometimes cross them with orange-eyed whites. Quite often one of the kittens in the resulting litter will have one eye which is deep blue and the other which is a bright orange.

# How to make a cat survey

You can find out which kinds of cats are the most common in your neighbourhood by making your own survey. With the help of a street map, draw a plan of the area in which you live, marking in houses, roads and paths.

Walk around the area and look for cats at least once every day for a week. Mark on your map where you see each cat, using a different colour dot for each different kind of cat. Try to remember the cats you see so that you mark each cat down on your map once only.

Put coloured dots on the map to show where you saw each cat.

Make a chart like this, noting down the kinds of cats you see in your survey. The following pages show some of the most popular varieties. Which ones are the most common in your area?

## 2

Unusual features sometimes appear in kittens. Normally, the front paw has five toes and the hind paw has four, but up to three extra toes may be present. In the tail-less Manx cat, tail bones are actually missing.

## 3

When Siamese cats were first brought to Europe in the late 1800s, they were slightly cross-eyed and had kinks in their tails. These features were seen as faults by breeders, and as a result, they have been deliberately bred out.

# Cats to look for: Shorthairs

**Bi-coloured.** Coat is one plain colour and white, but not more than two-thirds of it should be coloured. Chest, chin, belly and front legs are usually white. Eyes are orange, copper or yellow.

**Russian Blue.** Grey-blue coat is thick and silky. Notice the large whisker pads. Bright-green, almond shaped eyes. A quiet voice.

**Cornish Rex.** Very short wavy coat with no guard hairs. Can be any colour. Whiskers are crinkled and broken. There is also a Devon Rex with the same coat, but larger eyes and very large ears.

**Abyssinian.** Coat is rabbit coloured all over (no stripes), each hair being ruddy brown with bands of black or brown. Almond shaped eyes. There is also a Red Abyssinian.

**Tortoiseshell and white.** Also called Calico. Distinct black and red patches on a white background. Orange, copper or hazel eyes.

**Manx.** Easily recognized because it has no tail. Coat can be any colour or pattern. Hindquarters are very high and hind legs are long.

**Brown Burmese.** Rich, dark seal-brown glossy coat, lighter on the chest and belly. Ears and mask may be slightly darker. Slanting yellow eyes.

**Siamese.** Cream or white coat with some darker shading, the colour of which depends on the colour of the points. Points can be seal, chocolate, blue, red, lilac, tabby or tortie (tortoiseshell). Eyes are clear blue in all varieties. Siamese cats have points because colour develops only in the cooler parts of the body: the ears, face, tail and limbs.

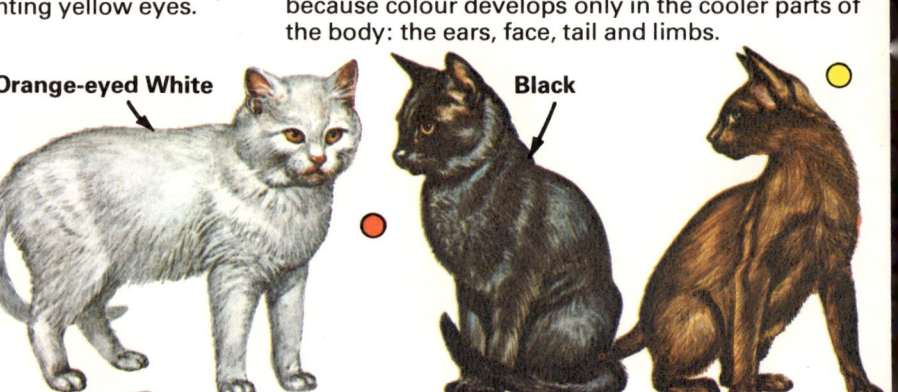

**Red Tabby.** Deep orange coat (not ginger) with distinct tabby markings of a darker red colour. There should not be any white. Hazel or orange eyes. Red tabbies are usually males. There is also a brown tabby shorthair.

**Silver Tabby.** Pure silver-grey coat with black tabby markings. These can be narrow (called mackerel) or wide (blotched). Green or hazel eyes.

**Orange-eyed White.** Pure white coat and deep orange or copper eyes. There are also blue-eyed and odd-eyed white shorthairs. **Black.** Another variety of self-coloured cat. Coat is jet black and eyes are deep orange or copper.
There are two other self-coloured shorthairs, one is called Blue and the other Cream.

**Havana.** Rich dark brown coat with no markings. Whiskers, nose and mouth are also brown. Large ears and a long tail. Green eyes.

● British or American shorthairs    ○ Foreign shorthairs

# Longhairs

The cats shown here are pedigree cats. Most of the cats you will see in your neighbourhood will probably be cross-bred or mongrel cats, but many of them may look similar to those shown here. The best place to see pedigree cats is a cat show.

**Colourpoint.** Cream or white coat with points like a Siamese, but the long hair and body shape of a Persian. The points can be different colours as with the Siamese. Blue eyes.

**Cream.** Long, silky, pure cream coloured coat, with short bushy tail and small tufted ears. Short thick legs. Large, round, deep copper coloured eyes.

**Brown Tabby.** Brown coat with black tabby markings. M-mark on forehead and bands around the legs and tail. Hazel or copper eyes. There are also red and silver longhaired tabbies.

**Turkish.** A semi-longhaired cat. Coat is chalk white with ginger markings on face and a ginger tail. Large upright ears. Amber coloured eyes. It is an unusual cat as it loves being in water.

**Black.** Pure black coat. Orange or copper eyes. Kittens may have a rusty black coat but as they get older, it changes to pure black. If a cat spends a lot of time in the sun, the coat may develop a brownish tinge.

**Smoke.** Silver neck ruff around a black face, with silver ear tufts. White undercoat. Top-coat is black on the back, shading to silver-grey on the sides of the body. Legs are black. Orange or copper eyes.

**Red Self.** You will not often see a cat with the correct coat colouring. It should be deep orange without tabby markings. Deep copper eyes.

**Chinchilla.** Undercoat is white, but each hair is tipped with black so the coat looks silver-grey. Skin on paw-pads and around eyelids is black. Eyes are emerald or blue-green.

**Orange-eyed White.** Pure white coat with no shading or marking of any kind. Brilliant orange or copper eyes. There are also blue-eyed and odd-eyed white longhaired cats.

**Seal-pointed Birman.** A semi-longhaired cat with creamy-brown coat and seal points. Easily recognised by the pure white socks on its feet. China blue eyes.

**Bi-coloured.** One plain colour and white, with not more than two-thirds of coat being coloured. Chin, chest, front legs and shoulders are white. Copper or orange eyes.

**Tortoiseshell.** Coat of black, red and cream in patches. Almost always females. Males are rare and are usually unable to mate successfully. Orange or copper eyes.

# Index

Abyssinian, **30**; Red, **30**.
ageing, **17**

Bi-coloured, **29**, **30**; Black and white, **30**, **31**; Cream and white, **31**; Red and white, **30**
Birman, **28**; Seal-pointed, **31**
birth, **19**, **20**
Black, **30**, **31**
Blue, **30**; Russian, **30**
body language, **9**
breeding, **28**, **29**
Burmese, Brown, **30**

Calico, *see* Tortoiseshell and white
carnivore, **4**, **10**
carrying basket, **24**, **27**
cat flap, **25**
catnip mouse, **25**
Cheetah, **4**
Chinchilla, **31**
claws, **6**, **7**, **8**, **9**, **11**, **21**, **22**
collar, **24**
Colourpoint, **31**; Seal, **31**
courtship, **18**
Cream, **30**, **31**
cross-breed, *see* mongrel

Dinictis, **4**
displacement activity, **13**
dog, **5**, **7**, **8**, **9**, **10**, **12**, **15**, **17**

ears, **4**, **7**, **9**, **12**, **14**, **24**, **26**, **28**
European Wild Cat, **4**
eyes, **4**, **7**, **9**, **17**, **21**, **24**, **28**

feeding, **7**, **20**, **21**, **23**, **24**, **26**
Felidae family, **4**
feline infectious enteritis, **24**
fighting, **12**, **13**, **19**
fleas, **26**, **27**
fur, **6**, **7**, **11**, **12**, **13**, **16**, **17**, **26**, **28**
fur balls, **16**

grooming, **7**, **12**, **13**, **17**, **22**, **23**, **27**

Havana, **30**
health, **24**, **25**, **26**
hearing, **10**, **15**, **21**
heat periods, **18**, **19**
hunting, **4**, **10**, **11**, **12**, **15**, **16**, **23**

illness, **27**
instinct, **10**, **14**, **16**

joints, **4**, **5**, **6**, **17**

kennels, **27**

language, **8**, **9**
learning, **14**, **15**, **16**, **23**
lifespan, **17**
Lion, **4**
longhair cats, **27**, **28**, **30**; *see also* individual breeds
Lynx, **4**

Manx, **29**, **30**
mating, **18**
Miacis, **4**
mites, ear, **26**
mongrel, **24**, **31**
mouse, **4**, **10**, **11**, **16**, **26**
muscles, **4**, **5**, **6**, **7**, **17**

neutering, **19**, **26**

paws, **6**, **7**, **9**, **11**, **12**, **22**, **29**
pedigree, **28**, **31**
Persian, **28**, **31**; Blue, **28**
playing, **7**, **12**, **17**, **22**, **23**, **25**; play-fighting, **13**; play-hunting, **10**
pregnancy, **18**, **19**, **20**
prey, **4**, **5**, **7**, **10**, **11**, **12**
pure bred cats, **24**, **28**

Rex, Cornish, **30**; Devon, **30**

Sabre-toothed Tiger, *see* Smilodon
scent glands, **8**, **9**
scratching post, **25**
season, in, **18**
Self, **28**, **29**, **30**; Red, **3**, **31**
semi-longhair cats, **28**, **31**
sexing kittens, **19**
shorthair cats, **27**, **28**, **30**; British or American, **28**, **30**; Foreign, **28**, **30**; *see also individual breeds*
shows, **24**, **31**
Siamese, **29**, **31**; Seal-pointed, **2**, **28**, **30**; Tabby-pointed, **30**
sight, **10**
"sixth sense", **14**
skeleton, **5**
skull, **4**, **5**
sleep, **12**, **21**, **22**
smell, sense of, **8**, **10**, **14**, **17**, **18**, **22**
Smilodon, **4**, **5**
Smoke, **31**
spaying, **19**
spraying, **8**, **18**, **19**
stray cats, **26**
suckling, **20**, **21**, **22**

Tabby, **28**, **29**; Brown, **28**, **31**; Red, **30**; Silver, **2**, **30**
tail, **5**, **7**, **9**, **13**, **23**
"talking", **8**, **9**
teeth, **4**, **5**, **7**, **9**, **11**, **12**, **17**, **21**, **24**; milk, **22**, **23**
territory, **8**, **12**, **13**, **15**, **18**
toilet tray, **23**, **24**
tongue, **7**, **12**
Tortoiseshell, **31**
Tortoiseshell and white, **30**
toys, **24**, **25**
training, **25**, **26**
travelling, **27**
Turkish, **28**, **31**

vaccination, **24**, **25**
vet, **20**, **24**, **25**, **26**, **27**

washing, **7**, **12**, **16**, **17**, **23**
weaning, **22**, **23**, **24**, **26**
weight, **26**
whiskers, **7**, **9**, **17**
White, Blue-eyed, **28**, **30**, **31**; Odd-eyed, **28**, **30**, **31**; Orange-eyed, **28**, **30**, **31**
worms, **26**

## Books to read

*Practical Guide to Cats.* Ivor Raleigh, Patricia Scott and Elizabeth & Oliphant Jackson (Hamlyn). A good general book on breeds of cats and cat care.
*Your Guide to Cats and Kittens.* Editor Ruth Gardiner (Peter Way). A good book with lots of useful information on looking after cats.
*Cats and Kittens.* Jane Rockwell (Franklin Watts). Fairly small children's book with sections on illness and showing your cat.
*Cats.* Grace Pond and Angela Sayer (Bartholomew). Cheap book with useful information on cat care and breeds.
*Cats . . . their health and care* by the TV Vet (Farming Press). Detailed but useful reference book, well illustrated with photographs.
*The Language of Your Cat.* Frank Manolson (Marshall Cavendish). A very interesting book about cats' behaviour with lots of photographs.
*Cats of the World.* Matt Warner (Bantam). A good book for identifying breeds. Very cheap and has colour photographs.
*The Observer's Book of Cats.* Grace Pond (Warne). Good for identification, with some general information as well.
*The Complete Cat Encyclopedia* edited by Grace Pond (Crown). Very large book with lots of information about all the cat breeds and also cat clubs and shows.
*The Wonderful World of Pets.* (Orbis). A very large book, worth getting from the library. Lots of sections on cats and cat breeds. Good colour photographs.

## Going further

If you are interested in finding out more about cats, it is best to go to a few cat shows. You will find details of shows in many cat and pet magazines, or you can look for advertisements in local newspapers. Alternatively, any library should be able to tell you the name and address of the central organization to which you can go for information.

At a show you will be able to ask about cat clubs. If you see one particular variety of cat you like, speak to a person showing one of those cats. You can join a club even if you have a mongrel cat, and some people join a club without even having a cat. All clubs have regular meetings with guest speakers. By going to these meetings you will learn much more about how to look after your cat properly.